# CAREERS IN

# HUMAN RESOURCES

## PERSONNEL MANAGEMENT

HUMAN RESOURCES MANAGEMENT, also known as HRM or simply HR, is the process of hiring and developing employees so that they become valuable members of the employer's organization. Any company, large or small, depends upon its employees for success. Human resources managers are the people in charge of ensuring that the right employees are recruited, hired, and trained. HR managers also serve as a vital link between an organization's management and its employees, often consulting with top executives on strategic planning.

The responsibilities of human resources managers fall into three major areas: staffing, employee compensation and benefits, and defining work. Their main job is to coordinate an organization's workforce, from planning personnel needs to hiring and firing. Depending on the size of the organization, they may also establish workplace policies, serve as the go-to person for questions about benefits, settle disputes among staff, evaluate worker performance, negotiate contracts, handle employee relations, develop training programs, and oversee other human resources staff. In essence, the purpose of all of these tasks is the same: to maximize the success of an organization by optimizing the effectiveness of its employees.

Many human resources positions require at least a bachelor's degree. A master's degree may be needed to secure a position as a specialist or to advance to a higher-level management position. It is also possible to get started with no college at all. Some entry-level jobs require only a high school diploma and a willingness to take on administrative duties as an assistant.

There is no single pathway to a career in human resources. Indeed, HR professionals come from a variety of backgrounds. Some have worked their way up the corporate ladder from clerical positions into management. Others set out to become HR managers and launch their careers directly from college. Some have transitioned into HR from other fields, such as finance, law, or technology.

One of the best aspects of this career is the wide variety of work settings. Wherever there are employees, there are HR professionals. That includes every industry, plus government agencies and nonprofit organizations. Wherever you choose to work, you can be sure that human resources management is a highly valued position. Business leaders understand that there is a higher risk of failure without a good HR manager to help attract and retain the best employees possible. In fact, HR managers are usually considered at the same level as executive officers, and are often included in major corporate decisions.

HR professionals agree that this is very satisfying work. The pay is good, but that is just the beginning. The job market is growing, working conditions are excellent, and layoffs are nearly unheard of. Best of all, there is no stress. The work is interesting, challenging, and rewarding. Human resources is a good choice for a person who wants to help people be more productive and fulfilled during their time spent in the workplace. If you want the chance to lead and, are eager to take on management responsibilities, take a closer look at this career.

## WHAT YOU CAN DO NOW

HUMAN RESOURCES MANAGERS ARE ALMOST always college graduates. Contact different colleges to learn what high school classes will be required for admission. In addition to those courses, your guidance counselor can help you design the best curriculum to prepare you for this career. In general, you will want to load up on math and business, especially statistics, accounting, and any management classes that are available.

Communications skills are especially important in this field. Look for any class or activity that puts you in front of a group of people. Take public speaking classes, get on the debate team, or join the drama club.

Develop your people skills. Does your school offer opportunities in peer tutoring? If so, seriously consider getting involved as a volunteer to gain experience dealing with other students one-on-one. It is an excellent way to develop the kinds of interpersonal skills you will need in your future career. Hone your leadership skills by running for a student government office or acting as president of a club.

Find out whether this career is right for you. Talk to people who are actually working in the field. Call up some local employment agencies and arrange to job shadow for a day or two. Being on the job with an HR professional is the best way to learn what to expect.

Seek out part-time work or a summer job at an employment agency. It is a good way to learn about your future clients' concerns and what you might be doing to help them.

Throughout your career, you will need to keep up on the latest techniques and employment trends. Start getting up to speed now by reading professional publications, such as *HR Magazine* or *Workforce Magazine.*

## HISTORY OF THE CAREER

UP UNTIL THE 18TH CENTURY, WORKING arrangements between employers and their workers were relatively simple. Within the framework of the guild system, which lasted for six centuries, an employer was a master craftsman who hired a young worker who would train as an apprentice. The apprentice lived with his master, and the master took care of his health and welfare.

Human resources management has since evolved and gained importance with each passing age. The history of modern human resources management started with the Industrial Revolution. In the 18th century, large factories were built, and they displaced the cottage-based guild manufacturing model. The priority for most industries shifted from hand-made quality to quick and cheap production. This new approach changed the world of work dramatically. Factories hired workers by the thousands with little regard to skills and experience, much less job satisfaction and decent working conditions. Long hours and unsafe conditions in factories led to labor riots, and the government started to intervene for the first time with laws to provide basic workers' rights and protections. Though unhappy with having to comply with regulations, employers came to realize that satisfied employees were more productive than unhappy workers. As a result, employers began to voluntarily introduce programs designed to increase comfort and satisfaction for their workers.

The beginning of the 20th century saw rapid development of human resources. The National Cash Register Company (NCR) created the first personnel management department after a contentious strike and lockout in 1901. The department's purpose was to address grievances, safety, dismissals, inaccurate record keeping, and court cases. Soon after, other large companies followed suit with the establishment of similar personnel departments. The personnel departments of the early 20th century were developed primarily for the benefit of the employer, a device used to ensure maximum productivity.

Focus on employee productivity continued in the wake of World War I, the Great Depression, and World War II. The demands of wartime production led to temporary relaxation of regulations. Keeping factories running at full tilt was more important than addressing issues of wages or working conditions.

With most men away at war, the landscape of the workplace changed. The workforce began to include women and people of all ages and ethnicity. This new multicultural workforce generated new challenges for personnel management. Trade unions evolved during this time, making it necessary for employers to deal with a strong partner rather than relatively weak individuals. Unions grew in size until the government eventually had to step in to limit the misuse of power. In 1947, the Taft-Hartley Act prohibited the use of "closed shops" that would only hire workers from a union. The law also gave the government jurisdiction over union mediation and management disagreements.

In the aftermath of World War II, America's population and workforce ballooned. It was the era of the Baby Boomer. This generation was the biggest in history and perhaps the most influential. Baby Boomers were also the most educated workers the US had ever seen, interested in ideas such as human rights and self-fulfillment. Integration of these concepts marked a distinct change in human resources management. On the legislative side, for example, there were numerous labor laws enacted, including the Equal Pay Act of 1963, the Civil Rights Act of 1964, the Occupational Safety and Health Act of 1970, and the Employee Retirement Income Security Act of 1974.

In the 1970s, technology and globalization brought more changes to the human resources arena. Economies shifted towards services and away from manufacturing. Instead of focusing on factory turnout, quality of services became the all-important competitive advantage. Yet keeping employees happy, whether in a factory or a call center, was still the key to meeting organizational goals. It became clear that people were the greatest asset of any organization. This concept was described in a nutshell in the Matching Model (also known as Hard HRM). Proposed by Fombrun, Tichy, and Devanna of the Michigan School of Business in 1984, this first formal HR model defined employees as a valuable resource to be obtained, developed, and exploited for the benefit of the organization.

The 1990s saw a major trend emerge where employees sought more balance between work and personal life. In most cases this meant seeking flexible scheduling. At the same time, the Internet had created a 24/7 world where the traditional 9-to-5 workday was no longer necessary nor desirable in many cases. An increasing number of employees wanted hours more conducive to raising a family, having personal time to work out at a gym, or just avoid the headaches associated with rush hour commutes. As a result, there was a marked rise in the number of part-time and temporary contracts, as well as more innovative solutions such as job sharing. There was also more potential for employees to work where they wanted. Technology made it possible for them to work from home or at any distant location. While a boon to employees, these changes radically altered ways of doing business and created new challenges for HR professionals to quantify and manage.

In just 100 years, human resources management has changed dramatically. The attitude of the early 1900s saw workers as replaceable cogs in the industrial machine. Today, highly educated workers control the machines. Employers understand that their competitive advantage is dependent on the skill of such workers. It is up to the human resources department to find them, hire them, and retain them. The work itself has evolved from hanging out "help wanted" signs and weekly paychecks, to facilitating a conducive work environment, enriching the worker's personal life as well as professional life, and encouraging loyalty through a myriad of innovative benefits.

## WHERE YOU CAN FIND WORK

THERE ARE ABOUT 100,000 HUMAN resources managers employed in the US today. They can be found working in virtually every industry, but the most common employers of HR managers are:

Company management firms

- Manufacturers

- Government agencies

- Administrative and support services

- Professional, scientific, and technical services

- Healthcare and social assistance organizations

- Finance and insurance firms

The largest number of salaried jobs is in the private sector, including part-time and self-employed workers. More than eight out of 10 HR managers work for non-governmental organizations. The rest, almost 20 percent, work in various government agencies, from local to state to federal levels. The work of government HR resources managers is often similar to those in the private sector. They also handle job classification, salary administration, government benefits, employee relations, and other matters related to public employees.

# Specialists

Human resources specialists and labor relations managers are also found working in nearly every industry. There are about half a million of these kinds of jobs in the US. Most, almost 85 percent, of those employed are human resources specialists. The others are labor relations specialists.

Human resources specialists are most often found working in the employment services industry. That includes employment placement agencies, temporary help services, and professional employer organizations. Many HR specialists are contract workers rather than salaried staff employees. That is because hiring needs in many industries fluctuate seasonally or rise and fall throughout the year. Therefore, organizations find it more efficient to contract outside HR firms to handle recruitment and placement rather than keep full-time specialists on staff permanently. It is common for HR specialists to be self-employed, working as consultants to private and public employers.

Labor relations specialists usually work for labor unions and other kinds of labor organizations. Only about 25 percent work for other types of employers.

Human resources managers spend most of their working time in offices that are modern, clean, and comfortable. For many, there is travel involved. Some HR managers work for large organizations with offices nationwide. They must travel to visit other branches and attend professional meetings. Human resources specialists, training specialists, and labor relations managers also travel extensively. Recruiters, in particular, travel far and wide to find potential candidates. They visit college campuses, attend job fairs, and interview prospective new employees in their hometowns. Arbitrators and mediators often work out of their homes, but they too need to travel to the sites chosen for negotiations.

## Work Schedules

Most human resources managers work full time during normal business hours. Workweeks are typically the standard 35 to 40 hours. For most, there is not much overtime involved. Fewer than one third work more than 40 hours a week. HR specialists, labor relations managers, arbitrators, and mediators are the most likely to experience longer hours. For example, when contract agreements are being prepared, time is of the essence. Negotiations are often delicate matters that need to continue uninterrupted until all parties are in agreement. In these instances, it may be necessary to work late into the night or continue on weekends.

---

## THE WORK YOU WILL DO

HUMAN RESOURCES MANAGERS HELP organizations attract, motivate, and retain qualified employees. Their work involves matching candidates with jobs for which they are well suited, overseeing employee relations, managing payroll and benefits, and leading employee training programs.

Human resources managers can generally be divided into two groups: generalists and specialists. The responsibilities of HR generalists can vary widely, depending on their organization's needs. These HR professionals typically do the following:

Help employers determine current and future employment needs

- Find, select, and hire qualified candidates for open positions

- Interview applicants and screen them according to experience, education, and skills

- Discuss job details with applicants including duties, working conditions, and compensation

- Contact references and perform background checks on job applicants

- Conduct new employee orientation

- Maintain personnel records and process paperwork

Generalists usually work in small organizations, utilizing their extensive knowledge of human resources to handle all the different job functions from recruiting to compensation. Specialists typically work for larger organizations, though a smaller employer may need to call in a consultant to provide specific expertise on a particular human resources specialty.

In a large organization, human resources activities are divided among a number of managers. Each will have a specific job to do, which may be recruitment, compensation and benefits, training and development, labor relations, or some other employment-related area. The managers who perform these jobs may be generalists with a broad knowledge of human resources, or they may be highly trained specialists focusing on a very specific function.

In a very large organization, there will be a director of human resources in charge of several departments. Each department will be led by an experienced manager, typically a specialist skilled in one type of employment activity, such as employee benefits or dispute resolution.

Large organizations are always looking to improve productivity and limit job turnover – both of which can have a profound effect on the bottom line. They depend on HR managers to help them make the best use of employee skills, provide training opportunities to enhance those skills, and boost employee satisfaction with their jobs and working conditions.

## Recruiters

Recruiters, sometimes known as staffing managers, are the lifeblood of the department. Their task is to find and hire the best candidates for job openings in an organization. They must be thoroughly familiar with the organization and its personnel policies in order to discuss with prospective employees issues of compensation, working conditions, and opportunities for promotions. Basic tasks involve screening, interviewing, checking references, administering any required pre-employment tests, and extending job offers.

To be successful in this position, a recruiter first must be able to find qualified applicants. This usually starts with posting job openings on electronic job boards, on the organization's website and Facebook page, and in various publications. Good recruiters seek to maintain contacts within the community, using networking techniques to fill positions (often long before they are advertised to the public). Depending on the size of the organization, recruiters may travel extensively, typically visiting college campuses and attending job fairs in search of promising candidates.

## Payroll Managers

Payroll managers oversee the operations of an organization's payroll department, making sure that employees are paid correctly and on time. In smaller organizations, they do it all – administer payroll procedures, prepare reports for the accounting department, and resolve any problems or discrepancies.

In larger organizations, there may be specialists known as compensation managers who are responsible for setting up and maintaining the firm's pay system. In order to ensure pay rates that are both fair and competitive, they do regular research within their industry and geographic location. They may periodically conduct surveys to compare their pay rates with other firms. They are also responsible for ensuring that their organization's pay scale complies with new laws and regulations. Some compensation managers are asked to establish and manage a performance evaluation system, which may include bonus programs or pay-for-performance plans.

## Benefits Managers

Employee benefits managers handle employee benefits programs. This has become an increasingly important area, as employers are paying more and more to provide benefits in order to attract and retain quality employees. The cost of providing benefits has been growing steadily and has become a significant proportion of overall compensation costs – more than 30 percent on average. Employee benefits managers have the knowledge and expertise to design and administer the most cost-effective, yet appealing benefits packages.

The basic employee benefits package consists of health insurance, sick leave, vacation time, and retirement plans. Familiarity with healthcare benefits is a top priority, due to the rapidly rising cost of healthcare coverage for employees and retirees. Most benefits packages go well beyond the basics, with benefits growing in number and complexity. Fewer and fewer retirement plans, for example, are traditionally defined pensions plans. Today's retirement plans typically include 401(k) plans (both employer matching and non-contribution), Individual Retirement Accounts (IRAs), Keoghs, ROTH plans, savings and thrift plans, stock ownership plans, and profit sharing. These are all complex strategies, which require in-depth knowledge and expertise on the part of the plan manager.

Some relatively new benefits have been introduced, reflecting the needs of the changing workforce. These include choices like parental leave (for both parents and adoptive parents), child and elder care, long-term nursing home care, wellness programs, transportation assistance, domestic partner benefits, and flexible benefits plans.

## Training and Development Managers

Training and development managers are specialists who conduct and supervise training and development programs for employees. On a daily basis, they conduct orientation sessions and arrange on-the-job training for new employees. They also utilize their special expertise in advanced learning theory to design programs that will increase productivity, improve the quality of work, help employees develop new skills, boost company morale, and build loyalty to the organization. Trainers also develop and oversee programs designed to help employees with transitions during mergers and acquisitions, or due to major technological changes.

Training and development managers also work with management. For example, they may teach supervisors how to improve their interpersonal skills in order to deal more effectively with their staff. In larger organizations, training specialists often set up leadership or executive development programs for employees in lower level positions. The purpose of these programs is to avoid gaps in leadership by preparing potential executives to replace those who are retiring.

## Labor Relations

Labor relations specialists, also known as employee relations representatives, negotiate and administer labor agreements. They usually work in agencies and companies employing union members, but they may also oversee employment policies in non-union settings. Their expert knowledge of legislation, labor law, economic and wage data, and collective bargaining trends makes them highly qualified to consult with both managers and employees during contract negotiations.

During the collective bargaining process, labor relations specialists draft informal language that will cover issues such as wages, benefits, grievances, healthcare, pensions, employee welfare, management practices, and other contractual stipulations. When all parties agree, they then draft the formal language that will seal the collective bargaining deal.

Labor relations specialists may also have these roles:

- Lead informal meetings between management and labor

- Interpret new labor laws, regulations, or precedents

- Advise management on disciplinary procedures

- Investigate the validity of labor grievances

- Train management on labor relations practices

- Analyze records of past union activity to anticipate future demands

- Promote the use of public employment programs and services

## Dispute Resolution

Dispute resolution has become an increasingly important and complex area in human resources. Human resources specialists with exceptional knowledge and experience work to achieve and maintain informal and contractual agreements between employees, management, unions, other organizations, and government agencies. Specific points of contention vary, but generally the goal is always to avoid costly litigation, strikes, and other damaging disruptions.

Dispute resolution specialists may have specific job titles that describe their area of expertise. For example, mediators (sometimes known as conciliators) are dedicated to advising and counseling both management and labor to prevent and resolve disputes over labor agreements. Arbitrators act more as referees during negotiations over labor contracts. Arbitrators are usually given the final say in whether any particular terms and conditions will be binding.

## Human Resources Assistant

There is a great deal of paperwork and computerized record keeping involved in human resources. At a minimum, the personnel records of an organization's employees contain contact information, earnings and benefits, job performance, attendance records, and tax withholding.   It is the job of the human resources assistant to maintain and update these records on a daily basis. For example, when an employee receives a promotion or wants to switch health insurance plans, the assistant must record the changes and update any relevant forms.

To some degree, human resources assistants may be involved in hiring. They may screen job applicants to assure all hiring criteria are met. They administer pre-employment tests, explain the organization's employment policies, and request and check references from past employers. It is often the assistant who informs applicants of their acceptance or rejection for employment.

In smaller organizations, responsibilities can cover a wide variety of duties. Human resources assistants answer phones and written inquiries, post announcements of job openings, issue and file applications, and organize examinations. When credit bureaus, lenders, and landlords request verification of employment, it is the human resources assistant who retrieves the authorized information from personnel records.

In larger organizations, human resources assistants have specific jobs. For example, they may be responsible for keeping track of upcoming vacancies and getting the word out to current employees about possible promotions or transfers. In a government setting, an assistant may be responsible for security matters, such as preparing and issuing passes, badges, and identification cards.

---

# HUMAN RESOURCES PROFESSIONALS TELL THEIR OWN STORIES

## I Manage the Recruitment Division of an Aerospace Company

"My job is to find and retain great employees for my company. About half of them are recent graduates whom I found while traveling to college campuses and participating in job fairs. The others were already employed by other companies. I only pursue the most talented that I think would be an ideal fit here.

I spend a lot of time traveling, which is something I enjoy. I love meeting new people, especially smart young people who are eager to make the transition from school to career. They inspire me. When not traveling, I train the recruiting staff on interviewing techniques, lead practice sessions in negotiations, and oversee intake procedures.

In the office and out, I have a lot of autonomy and freedom to do things as I see fit. Running a department of this size is a lot of responsibility, but there is surprisingly little stress involved. My colleagues in other departments are constantly up against deadlines and dealing with other short-term issues. My work is focused on longer-term goals. I may be recruiting for positions that aren't yet open or will eventually be needed, but don't even exist yet. There is never a rush, so I can take my time to find exactly the person we need to keep on hold.

There is very little I would change about my job. Every day is satisfying. I enjoy a six-figure salary and all the perks that go with it. I am especially pleased with the lifestyle. I have achieved a good balance between my personal life and my work. Even though I spend time on the road, there is plenty of time for my family and myself.

Prospective human resources managers should consider college majors carefully. The best college majors are in business, human resources, or communications. Regardless of your major, it is extremely important that you develop strong writing and speaking communications skills. There are numerous ways to acquire those skills beyond the usual coursework. You also need to be a people person. If you don't truly enjoy meeting and talking to people, this is not the career for you. If you are socially outgoing, that's a good sign. Being social and being able to read people are invaluable in a position that requires you to make value judgments on people you have just met."

# I Help People Do the Best Possible Job

"I was attracted to this field because I was intrigued by what makes people tick, particularly while they are at work. What motivates them to do their best versus just put in time on the clock? That is a question I strive to answer every day now. I majored in business management, but my favorite classes dealt with the psychology of people in organizations. I now use what I learned in those classes every day.

I am part of a team of training and development specialists. We work closely with company supervisors and department heads to get their new recruits off to a good start and then stay on track. I have helped develop numerous training programs, from new hire orientations, to strategic mentoring programs for future executives, to new technology implementation seminars. The most interesting part of my job is determining why people are not working well or not delivering what they are supposed to. It's my job to find ways to help that employee to improve. Sometimes that means retraining the managers to train their people properly. Other times it means the employee is in the wrong position. Maybe the position changed or maybe the person changed. Either way, I can get creative and find a solution.

The best thing about my job is being able to make a real difference to the environment that people work in. People spend more than half their waking lives in the workplace – sometimes much more. If they are stressed and feeling unappreciated, it spills over into their personal lives. It also makes them less effective employees. It can even make them sick. It is better for everyone if people are satisfied and fulfilled at work. A happy employee is a more productive, loyal employee. I get my own fulfillment and satisfaction from making an impact on how satisfied people are during their time at work.

Anyone considering human resources management shouldn't be put off by the amount of education that might be needed. There is a lot to learn, but the most important skills won't come from any book or classroom. Are you a good listener? Good communications is vital in this job. You also need tons of energy and a positive attitude. This is also a great choice for multitaskers who know how to organize their time without losing track of important details. So don't worry about the education. You can always get the knowledge you need, whether in school or on the job. I had to work hard to finish my education as I was working part time to fund my studies. It wasn't easy, but it was certainly worth it.

My advice to prospective HR professionals is to find a way to test drive the job. Get a summer job as an intern or an assistant. Or volunteer your time in a nonprofit's personnel department. Then make the most of every opportunity to learn new things. I got to know as much as I could about the field by watching others and asking questions."

## PERSONAL QUALIFICATIONS

WHEN HUMAN RESOURCES PROFESSIONALS interview new job candidates, they carefully evaluate how each potential employee stacks up against a list of key skills and personal characteristics needed for the job. But what happens when the tables are turned? What essential attributes do employers look for in human resources managers? In general, HR managers must be able to function under pressure, deal with conflicting points of view, be discreet and fair, and possess a persuasive yet congenial personality. You will need to demonstrate discretion, integrity, and fair-mindedness. There are also some personal traits that set successful HR professionals apart. The most common of these include the following:

## People Skills

Human resources is all about people. HR professionals interact with people on a daily basis, making interpersonal skills the number one qualification employers look for. The growing diversity of the workforce necessitates being able to work with people from various cultural backgrounds, levels of education, and experience. The best HR managers are able to assess whether a potential new hire is worth pursuing within minutes of meeting for the first time. This is an invaluable skill! Human resources professionals often work on teams to develop and implement strategies. The ability to maintain positive working relationships with colleagues is key to achieving successful outcomes. It is not just about cooperation though, it is about leadership. The best HR managers are natural leaders who are able to motivate and inspire people.

## Excellent Communications Skills

HR managers are often speaking for others, acting as the voice for management or on behalf of employees. They routinely communicate with management and all levels of employees, both current and potential. Communications are sometimes written, as in the case of employee performance reports. More often, it is speaking skills that count. HR managers routinely give presentations to department heads and speak to small and large groups in the community, on college campuses, and at job fairs around the country. Strong speaking skills are essential for managers to clearly describe their organizations and the available jobs within them. Listening skills are also important, particularly when interviewing and evaluating job applicants.

## Decision-Making Skills

Human resources managers are constantly making decisions. They decide whether to hire or fire employees on a daily basis. They also make decisions that will have a significant impact on employees and the organization. Such is the case when they are attempting to resolve labor disputes or worker grievances. It can be a delicate balancing act between protecting individuals and preserving the organization's culture and values. The best HR professionals are able to instill trust and confidence so that decisions are accepted as being in the best interest of all concerned.

## Organizational Skills

The world of human resources can be a whirlwind, changing from one minute to the next. On a typical day, an HR manager will deal with everything from an employee's personal issues to creating social media campaigns. HR managers must be able to prioritize and manage several projects at once without letting something critical slip through the cracks. It is a job that requires an orderly approach, strong time management skills, and personal efficiency. At the same time, it is important to stay flexible and able to move from one kind of task to another.

# ATTRACTIVE FEATURES

OVERALL, MOST HUMAN RESOURCES professionals are happy with their career choice. They enjoy interacting with people each day and find satisfaction in knowing their work directly affects people in a beneficial way. It is also a field that offers variety, good pay and benefits, and regular working hours. Here are some more reasons HR managers love what they do.

### The Work Is Interesting

There is constant variety in daily assignments and there is always something new to learn. You will never get bored because every day is different. Human resources managers interact with diverse groups of very talented business people at all levels of the organization. In most cases, they work with people in all the different departments. That might mean you interact with the production team one week and the sales team the next week. Along the way, you will be dealing with individuals – no one person is the same, which makes it all the more interesting.

People who work in human resources are vital to the health of the business. They can make a real impact on an individual, a team, or even the entire organization. For example, you might study how to minimize overhead costs without losing valuable staff. Based on your research, you then implement these changes and save your company millions of dollars. Being able to produce that kind of positive outcome can be extremely rewarding.

There is plenty of room to grow in this career. Even at the entry level, you are given serious responsibility and accountability. You can expect to be encouraged to be creative, share ideas, and add value to the business as a member of the team.

## UNATTRACTIVE ASPECTS

FOR MOST HUMAN RESOURCES PROFESSIONALS, the advantages far outweigh any drawbacks. The benefits are clear, but no career is perfect. Here are just a couple of the negatives you can expect to encounter when you enter this field.

Human resources professionals take on great responsibility. Most of the time, you will be able to easily handle what comes your way, and the people you are working with will be happy. The services you provide may often be taken for granted by employees. Then you will be rewarded with big smiles and "Thank you!" for the job offer or a promotion.

When something goes wrong, this suddenly becomes a thankless job. You may have to disappoint a new hire who did not get a desired salary, or explain to a production worker why hours are being cut back. Being the one to deliver the news that someone is being fired is probably every HR manager's least favorite task. Even when there is a good justification for the termination, it can be hard emotionally. Dealing with unsatisfied employees can be stressful.

Depending on the position, the work can be tedious and boring. This is usually the case for those just starting out in the human resources department. Entry-level workers are typically given simple administrative tasks such as processing paperwork for new hires or entering résumés into an online database. Even experienced human resources professionals can get stuck with daily routines that are quite monotonous. For example, those who work in payroll departments spend more time dealing with computer records than interacting with real people. Some people like that sort of thing, but if you are not one of them you may wonder if you made the right career choice. Fortunately, this is a field that provides plenty of opportunity for variety and upward movement. If you view each assignment as an opportunity for learning and growth, you will be rewarded with more interesting roles.

## EDUCATION AND TRAINING

BECOMING A HUMAN RESOURCES MANAGER generally requires a combination of education and related work experience. Because of the diversity of duties and level of responsibility, the educational requirements for new hires varies considerably.

Although such opportunities are limited today, it is still possible to land a job without going to college. For example, a high school diploma is sufficient education to qualify for some interviewing and recruiting positions. Most organizations provide training programs for entry-level employees. The most common is simple on-the-job training where new workers learn the profession by performing administrative tasks. Typical duties may include entering personnel data into computer systems, answering the phone and handling routine questions, gathering information for a supervisor, and compiling employee handbooks. This is a good way for clerical workers to get started in the field and find opportunities for career advancement that might otherwise have required more education.

In more formal programs, workers attend company-sponsored classes to learn how to classify jobs, interview applicants, and administer employee benefits. Upon completion of the classes, the new hires are then assigned to specific areas in the HR department to gain experience. They may later advance to a managerial position, overseeing a major element of the personnel program. It may take several years to gain enough work experience to substitute for the lack of a college degree.

Another option for those who may not have the time or money to invest in a four-year college program is to obtain an associate degree. These two-year programs are available from many community colleges and vocational schools. They typically offer convenient scheduling with evening classes for students who may work full time during the day. Courses vary widely among associate degree programs. Human resources topics may cover personnel recruitment and evaluation, employment law, staff training, and compensation and benefits.

For most human resources management positions, employers prefer college graduates who have earned a bachelor's degree, especially those who have prepared for the field by majoring in human resources, personnel administration, or industrial and labor relations. Others may look for a technical or business background related to the employer's field, such as engineering, finance, or law. Also, many employers will accept a well-rounded liberal arts education.

Depending on the school, courses leading to a career in human resources management may be found in departments of business administration, education, instructional technology, organizational development, human services, communications, or public administration, or within a separate human resources school or department.

Courses for a human resources degree start with core business training in areas such as accounting, finance, information technology, and marketing. The third and fourth year curriculum focuses more on vocational HR topics, such as:

- Organizational theory and design

- Behavioral science

- Employment law and legal issues

- Performance management and assessment

- Employee training and development

- Compensation and benefits

- Industrial psychology

## Graduate Education

Although a bachelor's degree is sufficient for most positions, a master's degree is becoming increasingly important. Candidates for top management positions may qualify with either a master's degree in human resources or an MBA (Master of Business Administration) with a human resources focus. Either way, courses focus on in-depth HR concepts such as organizational psychology and design, ethical leadership, corporate business strategy development, leadership, and human resources subsystems.

## Certifications

Many employers prefer to hire certified candidates, and some positions may require certification. Although voluntary, certification can enhance a human resources professional career advancement opportunities by demonstrating knowledge and competence across a range of human resources topics. The most widely accepted certification programs are offered by two professional organizations: The HR Certification Institute and the International Foundation of Employee Benefit Plans. Some certificates are for generalists, such as the Professional in Human Resources. Others, like the Certified Employee Benefit Specialist, are designed for various types of HR specialists. All certifications require specific college-level coursework, relevant work experience, and a comprehensive exam.

## EARNINGS

HUMAN RESOURCES MANAGERS ARE paid well. Annual salaries average from $40,000 on the low end to more than $175,000. The median annual income for an HR generalist now hovers at just over $100,000.

Differences in earnings are due primarily to the level of education and years of experience the HR professional might have. To a lesser degree, pay rates vary among different types of employers. The median annual wages for human resources managers among the top five employment groups are as follows:

| | |
|---|---|
| Management of companies and enterprises | $113,000 |
| Professional, scientific, and technical services | $112,000 |
| Manufacturing | $ 98,000 |
| Government | $ 92,000 |
| Healthcare and social assistance | $86,000 |

Specialists usually earn more – about 10 percent more – than their generalist colleagues do. Again, this is mostly because these positions require more education and experience than a generalist might have. The two biggest and highest paying areas for specialists are training and development, and labor relations.

Salaries for human resources assistants also vary considerably depending on the location, size of city, industry, and size of organization. An assistant's level of expertise has little influence on earnings since most assistants move up the career ladder as they gain knowledge and experience.

Salaries for human resources assistants range between $35,000 and $45,000. The average nationwide is about $40,000 annually.

Median annual earnings among the largest groups of employers of human resources assistants are:

| | |
|---|---|
| Federal government | $42,000 |
| Business management firms | $39,000 |
| Local government | $36,000 |
| Accounting, tax preparation, and payroll services | $34,000 |
| Employment services | $33,000 |

The highest salaries are offered in the software publishing industry where human resources assistants are paid more than $55,000 on average. However, this is not only a relatively small industry with few opportunities, but also employers tend to be located in areas with a high cost of living.

Human resources professionals at all levels receive comprehensive benefits packages. Some employers also provide educational assistance to lower level workers such as human resources assistants who want to enhance their opportunities for advancement in the field.

## OPPORTUNITIES

THE NUMBER OF JOBS FOR HUMAN resources managers is expected to grow almost 15 percent over the coming decade. This pace is about average for all occupations. New HR jobs often come from increasing efforts to recruit and retain quality employees in order to compete. This is nothing new. What is new is the growing complexity of many jobs in all industries. An aging workforce combined with advancing technology is leaving many employees with obsolete skills. Employers are having to devote greater resources to job-specific training programs – the kind that HR managers specialize in developing.

Job opportunities should continue to be best among companies involved in management, consulting, and personnel supply of other firms. There has been a growing trend over recent years toward outsourcing human resources functions. Generalists and specialists are both being sought for temporary job assignments. Firms have determined that it is more cost effective to contract recruiters and interviewers as needed rather than having full-time salaried HR staff handle these basic tasks. About 15 percent of HR specialists work under contract in the employment services industry. Specialists most in demand are those in training and development, and employee benefits analysts. Temporary work is offered by both temporary and permanent staffing agencies.

Legislation concerning employment issues has long been a driving force behind the need for more human resources professionals. For example, the Affordable Care Act is one of the most significant forms of legislation affecting employers in decades. The adoption of the Act spurred the need for more HR managers to help implement the program. Court rulings continue to set new standards in a wide variety of employment areas such as equal employment opportunity, occupational safety and health, family leave, and pensions. Organizations have no choice but to keep up with the ever-changing, complex employment laws and regulations. This puts sharp human resources managers and labor relations experts in high demand.

There are numerous opportunities for human resources managers, but there is also competition for most positions. There is no shortage of qualified college graduates and experienced professionals. The key to gaining an edge over the competition is education. In general, candidates without a bachelor's degree and related work experience may have difficulty landing a good job quickly. Those with a master's degree and certification have the best job prospects.

Employment of human resources professionals will be somewhat weakened as companies use advanced technologies to increase efficiency and cut costs. For example, some firms have stopped sending recruiters to college campuses and job fairs in favor of conducting the entire recruiting and application process online. Job growth has also been tempered by the widespread use of human resources information systems. This is very efficient software that makes it easy to quickly process and manage personnel information. Because the HR workers using it are more productive, fewer of them are needed to get the job done.

Employment growth among human resources specialists varies by specialty. In the global economy, international human resources management is a hot area. Changing technology continues to open up more jobs for those who are experts in human resources information systems. Conversely, the prospects for labor relations specialists are likely to be less favorable. Companies do still need good arbitrators and mediators to resolve labor disputes and avoid costly court battles. However, most of these jobs have come from unions. Union membership has been declining in recent years, resulting in less need for these specialists to utilize their skills.

## GETTING STARTED

TODAY'S EMPLOYERS STRONGLY prefer candidates with experience. According to SHRM (Society for Human Resource Management), at least one year of experience is necessary to obtain even an entry-level job in human resources. Get as much experience as you can in as many areas as you can. Ideally, your experience will be in the HR department, but it is advantageous to understand the many aspects of business. If you have a job, offer to perform a wider variety of tasks and take on more roles to get a clearer view of what it takes to run a business.

Corporate recruiters visit college campuses to find new talent. Seek them out and try to get a job as a human resources assistant. Participate in any job fairs and check your school's career center often for new job postings.

If you cannot find a paying job, you can gain the experience you need through an internship or volunteer program. Even if you do not have the opportunity to intern through a college program, many large companies offer internships for students and recent graduates. In fact, this is the most common way for new graduates to get started in the field. According to an SHRM survey, almost all HR undergraduates stated that working as an intern provided essential preparation for entry-level HR jobs.

Consider graduate school. To advance beyond an entry-level job, experience and additional training may be necessary. Graduate courses can prepare you for a management position by teaching you techniques in strategic planning, contract negotiation, arbitration, and mediation. You can earn a master's degree in a broad discipline, such as organizational leadership, or choose to focus on a specialty such as personnel administration or industrial relations.

Look for human resources job posts on major sites like Monster, CareerBuilder and Indeed. Not having any luck? Give HR-specific job boards a try. A few to start with are SHRM's HR Jobs, HR Crossing, and HR.com Job Board.

Network, network, and network some more. Human resources management positions often get filled without ever being advertised. Whether you are just starting out or have years of experience under your belt, the best way to find job opportunities is to get out and look for them. Attend conferences, seminars, and other professional activities. Keep track of the people you meet. Do not just let the names take up space in your address book. The names are of no value until you actively cultivate them. Let people – particularly those in key positions – know what you can do and where you want to go next in your career.

Do your homework. Research the industries that interest you and learn all you can about the types of companies you would like to work for. Visit company websites and spend some time there. Read the mission statement, note the company culture, and keep current with their projects. When you find a particular company you would like to work for, use your networking skills to get the name of someone in that company who can open a door for you. Simply knowing a name or having a phone conversation is better than blindly sending your résumé, hoping it will not get lost in the pile.

## ASSOCIATIONS

■ **Society for Human Resource Management**
**http://www.shrm.org/pages/default.aspx**

■ **American Payroll Association**
**www.americanpayroll.org**

■ **Association for Talent Development**
**www.td.org**

■ **International Foundation of Employee Benefit Plans**
**http://www.ifebp.org**

■ **HR Certification Institute**
**http://www.hrci.org**

## PERIODICALS

■ **Workforce Magazine**
**http://www.workforce.com**

■ **HR Magazine**
**www.shrm.org/publications/hrmagazine/pages**
**/default.aspx**

## WEBSITES

■ **WorldatWork**
**http://www.worldatwork.org**

■ **HR.com**
**http://www.hr.com**

■ **HRCrossing**
**www.hrcrossing.com**

Made in the USA
Middletown, DE
28 December 2018